Business Funding & Finances

Young Adult Library of Small Business and Finance

Building a Business in the Virtual World

Business & Ethics

Business & the Government: Law and Taxes

Business Funding & Finances

Keeping Your Business Organized:
Time Management & Workflow

Managing Employees

Marketing Your Business

Starting a Business: Creating a Plan

Understanding Business Math & Budgets

What Does It Mean to Be an Entrepreneur?

Young Adult Library of Small Business and Finance

Business Funding & Finances

C. F. Earl

Mason Crest

Mason Crest
450 Parkway Drive, Suite D
Broomall, PA 19008
www.masoncrest.com

Printed in the United States of America.

First printing
9 8 7 6 5 4 3 2 1

Series ISBN: 978-1-4222-2912-5
ISBN: 978-1-4222-2915-6
ebook ISBN: 978-1-4222-8905-1

The Library of Congress has cataloged the
hardcopy format(s) as follows:

Library of Congress Cataloging-in-Publication Data

Earl, C. F.
   Business funding & finances / C.F. Earl.
      pages cm. – (Young adult library of small business and finance)
   Audience: Grade 7 to 8.
   ISBN 978-1-4222-2915-6 (hardcover) – ISBN 978-1-4222-2912-5 (series) –
ISBN 978-1-4222-8905-1 (ebook)
   1. Small business–Finance–Juvenile literature. 2. New business enterprises
–Finance–Juvenile literature. 3. Business enterprises–Finance–Juvenile literature. I. Title.
   HG4027.7.E23 2014
   658.15–dc23
                                        2013015649

Produced by Vestal Creative Services.
www.vestalcreative.com

CONTENTS

Introduction   6

1. You Need Money to Make Money   11

2. Personal Savings   25

3. Loans   35

4. Grants   47

Find Out More   58

Vocabulary   60

Index   62

About the Author and Consultant   63

Picture Credits   64

INTRODUCTION

Brigitte Madrian, PhD

Small businesses serve a dual role in our economy. They are the bedrock of community life in the United States, providing goods and services that we rely on day in and day out. Restaurants, dry cleaners, car repair shops, plumbers, painters, landscapers, hair salons, dance studios, and veterinary clinics are only a few of the many different types of local small business that are part of our daily lives. Small businesses are also important contributors to the engines of economic growth and innovation. Many of the successful companies that we admire today started as small businesses run out of bedrooms and garages, including Microsoft, Apple, Dell, and Facebook, to name only a few. Moreover, the founders of these companies were all very young when they started their firms. Great business ideas can come from people of any age. If you have a great idea, perhaps you would like to start your own small business. If so, you may be wondering: What does it take to start a business? And how can I make my business succeed?

A successful small business rests first and foremost on a great idea—a product or service that other people or businesses want and are willing to pay for. But a good idea is not enough. Successful businesses start with a plan. A business plan defines what the business will do, who its customers will be, where the firm will be located, how the firm will market the company's product, who the firm will hire, how the business will be financed, and what, if any, are the firm's plans for future growth. If a firm needs a loan from a bank in order to start up, the bank will mostly likely want to see a written business plan. Writing a business plan helps an entrepreneur think

through all the possible road blocks that could keep a business from succeeding and can help convince a bank to make a loan to the firm.

Once a firm has the funding in place to open shop, the next challenge is to connect with the firm's potential customers. How will potential customers know that the company exists? And how will the firm convince these customers to purchase the company's product? In addition to finding customers, most successful businesses, even small ones, must also find employees. What types of employees should a firm hire? And how much should they be paid? How do you motivate employees to do their jobs well? And what do you do if employees don't get along? Managing employees is an important skill in running almost any successful small business.

Finally, firms must also understand the rules and regulations that govern how they operate their business. Some rules, like paying taxes, apply to all businesses. Other rules apply to only certain types of firms. Does the firm need a license to operate? Are there restrictions on where the firm can locate or when it can be open? What other regulations must the firm comply with?

Starting up a small business is a lot of work. But despite the hard work, most small business owners find their jobs rewarding. While many small business owners are happy to have their business stay small, some go on to grow their firms into more than they ever imagined, big companies that service customers throughout the world.

What will your small business do?

Brigitte Madrian, PhD
Aetna Professor of Public Policy and Corporate Management
Harvard Kennedy School

ONE

You Need Money to Make Money

Successful business owners know that the old saying "Money doesn't grow on trees" is very true. They may be making a lot of money now, but they weren't when they first started out. In fact, those business owners had to spend money to start their businesses in the first place.

Businesses don't start out of nowhere. Someone has to think of a great business idea. Then she needs to make it happen. And part of making a business happen is financing it—putting some money into it. Just about every business needs a little money to get it off the ground.

There is no magical startup kit for your new business. Oftentimes, you'll have to make a lot of decisions on your own and find your own way to succeed.

Business Funding & Finances

Startup Costs

The things you'll need to pay for to start your business are called startup costs. Your business will cost you a little money to start running, before you even sell anything. Before you start your business, you should list everything you plan on doing. Then list what you'll need to buy to make each of those things happen.

Are you planning on building a website for your business? You may need to spend a little money first. You have the option of setting up a free website through sites like Wordpress. You also can get more serious and buy your own website domain name. Your domain name will be totally unique, and it will help people find your product or *service*. Buying a domain name will cost between $5 and $30. You'll probably also need to renew your domain name every year, to keep it up and running. You can use online registrars to find domain names that aren't already taken and buy them. Check out GoDaddy.com, Register.com, or 1&1 Internet.

You may also need to buy materials to make your product, if you happen to be selling a physical product. Paper, food, jewelry-making supplies—whatever it is, you'll need to buy materials before you can assemble and sell your products. If you're planning on designing computer applications, games, or programs, you might have to update your computer or buy new software.

To run a business, you might also need to apply for a license. Licenses are written permission to do something, usually given to you by the government. In a lot of towns, you'll need to get a business license to even run a business. Special businesses, like selling food, require more licenses. If you want to set up a real store, or sell things out of your house, you'll also need a license.

Business licenses can cost money, so do some research on which licenses you'll need and how much your town will charge you for them.

When you're just starting out, you don't know everything about running a business. You can ask for advice from knowledgeable people, like business owners you may know, or a business teacher at school. You also have the option of taking business classes. Community colleges and other organizations often offer short classes on how to run a business. The classes cost money, but they'll help you run your business smoothly and *effectively*.

Besides business classes, you may decide to take classes to learn more things so you can use your skills to sell stuff. You may really like the idea of selling pottery at craft fairs. The trouble is, you're not that good at pottery yet because you're just starting to learn. Taking a pottery class can speed up the process, and help you make bowls and mugs you're proud to sell.

Finally, there are a few costs you may have to think about if you're really serious about your business. Some business people want to start corporations. A corporation is a company that is independent of you. Corporations are almost like people. They pay *taxes*, have to pay *debts*, and can get punished for committing crimes. Whenever you see a business with a name that has an "Inc." on the end, that tells you the business is a corporation. ("Inc." is short for incorporated.)

Every state has different rules about forming a corporation, but you'll have to pay some money no matter where you live. You'll fill out some forms and pay anywhere from $100 to $800 to incorporate.

Another startup cost you may have if you're really serious about your business is renting a business location. You have the

option of running your business out of your home, which probably makes the most sense if you're a young person just starting out with a business. However, if you're already an experienced businessperson and you're ready to sell out of a store, you'll have to think about how much you'll pay to rent a store, as well as buy shelves, decorations, and office supplies.

Although a store is likely out of your reach right now, you might want to think about taking your business to a local farmers' market, selling at craft fairs, or running a table somewhere else in your town. You'd need to buy a table, signs, and a display. Then you'll be able to sell your products wherever you want.

Imagine you want to start a new business doing graphic design. You love playing around on the computer, designing websites and creating signs. Your school projects always look really great because you spend hours designing them on the computer. You're pretty sure you can turn your talents and hobby into a real business that makes you some money.

At first glance, a graphic design business doesn't seem like it would cost you much money to start, but you want to be sure. You start writing down all your startup costs. You list:

- a license to start a home-based business ($50)
- a domain name for your website ($15)
- a class you want to take on graphic design at a local community school ($150)

Altogether, you need $215 to get your business started.

Promoting your company website through search engines like Google is a great way to spread the word about your business, particularly in your company's early days.

Business Funding & Finances

PICKING THE RIGHT DOMAIN NAME

You might have to get creative when you come up with a domain name. The most obvious one might already be taken, because people have created so many websites already. You should think of a few key words that go with your business. You might have to use some of them if your business name is already taken. Some people suggest you stick to .com names, instead of .net or .org. People tend to assume all domain names are .com, so if you use another ending, your customers might get confused. Make your domain name easy to remember and easy to spell, so make it fairly short. Hyphens can make domain names confusing too. You don't want a name that is fifty letters long, because people won't remember it!

On-Going Costs

Besides your startup costs, your business will take more money just to keep going. On-going costs will be different from business to business. Like with startup costs, you want to write down all your on-going costs so you can keep track of them and remember you have to save some money to pay for them.

Just like you needed materials at the beginning, you'll need to keep buying materials to keep selling your products. Hopefully, you're selling enough so that you can pay for new materials. For example, if you're selling jewelry, you'll need to buy new beads, clasps, and chains every so often, so you can make more jewelry.

Advertising will cost you some money, too. As your business grows, you'll want to keep advertising so more and more people know about you and your business. You can buy advertising space in the newspaper or online, or you can print out your own flyers. Whatever choice you make, you'll pay a little bit of money. The more advertisements you post, the more it'll cost you.

Keeping your website up to date will also cost a little money. You usually have to renew your domain name every year, at the cost you spent to buy it in the first place. Don't forget to keep a little money aside to keep your website going.

A big on-going cost is going to be taxes. Every year, you'll need to pay *income* tax to the government. Income tax is tax on how much money you make with your business. After you make more than a certain amount as a *self-employed* worker, you'll have to pay taxes. The more money you make, the more you'll get taxed. Everyone who makes enough money has to help the government pay for things like roads, police, and schools. Instead of complaining, realize your business is doing well enough to start owing taxes!

So say your graphic design business has started out slow. A couple people hired you to do some website design, but you want more work. You realize you need to do some advertising. Luckily, your business is all about creativity and design, so you make some really amazing posters you hang up all over town. You decide to pay to get them printed at a printer, so they look *professional*.

The ads work! You suddenly have a lot more customers. By the end of the year, you made $700 with your graphic design business—not bad for your very first year. Your mom tells you you'll have to pay taxes, though. You and your mom do your research and fill out the right forms. You only have to pay a little tax for now. Your ongoing costs so far include advertising and taxes.

Making Money

The point of spending all this money is to make money! By setting up a good business to begin with, and spending a little money to keep it going, you're making sure your business is doing well.

Every time you spend money on your business, that money should help your business make more money. If you realize something you're spending money on is not helping your business do better, stop spending that money.

With your graphic design business, you realize you're doing well. You're getting new customers and making more money. However, you seem to be spending a lot of money on

MORE ON TAXES

Just about everyone who makes money has to pay taxes. You might think it's unfair that the government is taking away money you made by working hard, but taxes make sense if you think about them the right way. Part of the government's job is to provide services for its citizens. The government protects people with police forces, an army, and prisons. The government builds things like bridges, roads, parks, and subways. It pays for public schools so that all young people can have an education. The government does a lot of things for us, but all of those things cost money and aren't just free for us. We pay for them partly with taxes. So, the taxes you pay on the money you make go to pay for all those services, which help you out. They also help everyone else in the country.

advertisements. You're not sure it's worth it, so you look into how necessary your ads are.

You ask all your current customers how they found out about your business. Almost all of them say they heard about it by word-of-mouth. Someone they knew told them about your business, so they went ahead and got in contact with you. No one tells you they hired you because they saw an ad. You have enough loyal customers right now that you decide to stop printing and posting flyers. Maybe in the future you'll need to advertise more, but you can cut that out of your costs for now! You've just cut out a big on-going cost.

Balancing It Out

The most important things to do as a business owner is to stay organized. Write everything down, from your purchases, to whom your customers are, to how much money you're making.

As an organized businessperson, you'll want to make a budget. A budget is simply an **estimate** of how much you're going to spend on your business and how much you're going to make.

Before you even start selling anything, make a budget. List all your startup and on-going expenses. Using Excel or another computer spreadsheet program is often the easiest way to keep track of your business, but you can also do it on paper. Add up your expenses to see how much money you're spending on your business.

Then list how much money you think you'll make with your business. This is where you decide how much you want to charge for your service or product. Don't charge too much, or no one will want to buy from you. You also don't want to charge too little, or you'll be wasting an opportunity to make more money.

Your goal is to balance your budget (that is, come out even, so that you make as much money as you spend) or—even better—to make more money than you're spending. Making more money than your costs is your profit.

You estimated your startup costs for your graphic design business were $215. You're not sure exactly how much your on-going costs for your first year will be, but you guess you'll pay $100 in taxes, and $30 in advertising. In total, all your business costs are $345.

Your goal is to make at least $345. In your first year in business, making more than you're paying can be hard, so don't get frustrated! You might need a couple years to really get going and start making money.

To get to $345, you make a few calculations. First, you see how much you'd have to charge for each graphic design job if you only had three customers who wanted websites. Each customer would have to pay $345 ÷ 3, or $115. You don't think people will want to pay you that much, so you know you'll have to charge less. Charging less per job means you should aim to get more than three customers.

Next you calculate how much you could charge if you had twenty customers. That's $345 ÷ 20, or $17.25. Your time and skills are worth more than that! You'll need a few days to design each website, and you think you should make more than $17.25 for your time. You realize you should charge somewhere in between $17.25 and $115 for each website. In the end, you pick $50, which seems reasonable for you and your customers. At $50 per job, you'll need about seven customers to cover all your business costs. Seven customers also seems like a reasonable number.

Keeping your finances organized makes it easy to calculate your budget. An accurate budget will help you plan for the year ahead with confidence!

During the year, you keep track of how much each customer pays you. At the end of the year, you count up the total. You made $700 in all! You ended up with fourteen customers, who all paid $50 for a website design. You were such a good businessperson that you doubled your goal in money and in customers. You easily covered your costs, and you can see exactly how because you kept all your records organized. Now you're ready for your next business steps. Of course, your next steps will cost more money!

TWO

Personal Savings

So now you know that businesses cost money to start. The money you spend on them helps you make more money in the end. You may have spotted the missing step here—getting the money in the first place.

Money may not grow on trees, but there are plenty of places you can get some money to start a business. You sometimes have to be creative or take some risks, but if you're *passionate* enough, you'll usually be able to make it work!

One place you can find money is right in your bank account or piggy bank. As a young person, you may have a little money saved up. Maybe you're saving for a car, or for college, or just for some spending money. Starting a business can be a great use of your money, as long as you know the risks and make the right choices.

STARTING A BUSINESS STEP BY STEP

Starting a business can be a lot of work, but it's exciting and rewarding work! Here are a few steps to starting up a serious business.

1. Decide on your business. Ask yourself what you're good at and what you enjoy doing. Can you make your interests into a business that makes you money?
2. Research your competition. Figure out if other businesses are already selling what you want to sell, and if there's room for another similar business. Take a look at what similar businesses are charging their customers to figure out your own prices.
3. Name your business. Pick a name that is creative but still tells people plainly what your business does.
4. Create a business plan. Business plans are basically roadmaps for success—they cover what your business will be, and how you will run it.
5. Make a list of your expenses. What are the things you need to buy to start your business? Will you need materials, space, employees, or training?
6. Find money. You'll need money to cover all your expenses. You can spend your own money, or find people who are willing to give you a loan.
7. Advertise. Print out flyers, advertise in the newspaper, and use the Internet to spread the word about your business. Make sure your ads have enough information, including what you sell, how

much it is, and how to contact you. Get business cards and hand them out to people you meet.

8. Keep track of finances. Write down all the money you spend and the money you make. That way, you'll be able to see if you're making money.

9. Pay taxes. If you make enough money, you legally have to pay taxes. Check with the IRS (Internal Revenue Service) to figure out if you made enough to pay taxes.

Deciding to Use Your Money

Using your own money to pay for your business costs is fast and easy. You don't have to ask anyone permission, you don't have to pay anyone back, and you already have access to it.

Although using your own money is easy, you'll want to think really hard about whether or not you want to use it. After all, if you use your money for a business, you won't be able to use it to buy a bike or anything else you were saving up for.

On the other hand, one of the reasons you're starting a business in the first place is to make money. By paying for startup costs, you'll be giving yourself a chance to increase the money in your bank account by a lot!

In the end, you need to run a good business to reduce the risk of using your personal money. Starting an expensive business and then not making any money means you'll lose all the money you

Since you own your own business, all of the profit is yours. You could use this profit for something that you have been saving up for or you could invest this money in your business and see your profits grow even larger.

put into it. But paying for some startup costs and then making sure you make good business decisions will make it more likely that your business is successful. You'll end up with more money than you started out with. So do your research and ask around for advice. Figuring out how to do business will be a good learning opportunity, and will be good for your wallet.

Business Funding & Finances

How Much Should I Use?

Deciding to use some personal money is one thing. Deciding how much of your savings to use is another. Should you go ahead and put all the money you have into your business, to make it more successful? Or should you only use a little bit, but risk not covering all your startup costs?

The answer will be different for every young person starting a business. In general, using your entire life's savings is not usually the best idea. You want to keep some in case you really need it for something. However, as a young person, you probably don't need too much money for emergencies. You may be saving for a big purchase, though, like a car, computer, or college. You'll need to balance how much you want those things and how much you want your business to succeed.

One thing you can do is start saving for your business. You might have to put your business plans on hold for a little while if you don't have enough money to start right away. Instead, you can spend time planning for your business, so that when you start, you'll be all ready to go. In the meantime, save up!

If you don't already have a savings account, create one. Put the money you have into your account to keep it safe. Banks also give you *interest* on the money in your savings account. The interest isn't very much, but it's something. You'll get a little bit of money paid to you every month just for having money in a savings account. That little bit of money is more than you'd get if your money were just sitting at home.

Every time you get some money, put some in your savings account for your business. Add the check your grandma gave you for your birthday. Put in the money your neighbor gave you for

Combining her love of fashion, drive to succeed, and some money she had saved, by only fourteen Zoe Damacela was already making a profit!

walking his dog. If you have a part-time job, add your **wages** to your account. Before you know it, you'll have enough to start your business!

Business for Real

Zoe Damacela is a young businessperson who is making it big. Her fashion company, Zoe Damacela Apparel, has successfully been selling dresses and other clothes for several years. Zoe was a freshman in high school when she started her business. Pretty soon, she was selling dozens of dresses. Eventually, her business caught the eye of some big names. Zoe has appeared on *The Tyra Banks Show*, won *Seventeen* magazine's Pretty Amazing contest (and even appeared on the cover), and given a speech at the White House.

Zoe remembers what it was like when she was just starting out. In fact, fashion design wasn't her first business. She told the story of her first business in an interview. "I really wanted a Razor scooter," Zoe says. "All of my friends had one. My mom kept saying 'No. No. No. It's not your birthday.' She finally said, 'If you can raise half the money yourself I'll pay for the rest.' I think she said that just to get me to stop bothering her. I ended up making greeting cards and selling them around the neighborhood. Within a couple of hours I had enough money to buy my scooter." Zoe had business smarts even when she was eight. She learned how to make money with just a little **investment** of her own money.

By the time she was a teenager, she had saved up some money from her business adventures. Now it was time to try something even bigger. "[My mom] was very **adamant** about the fact that if I wanted to work and succeed, I had to do everything by

Zoe's sewing class was one of her start-up costs. "I always have loved arts and crafts," Zoe says. Refining those skills turned out to be very profitable for her!

Business Funding & Finances

myself," Zoe says. She paid her business startup costs herself, with the money she had saved. She took a sewing class, and used her sewing machine and new skills to start making clothes.

At first, Zoe sold her products cheaply. She sold dresses for $13. After a little while, she realized all her hard work and her creativity made the dresses worth a lot more. She now sells her dresses for hundreds or even thousands of dollars. Zoe explains that her business has "been profitable since I was fourteen. The secret is finding something you're really good at and that you really love."

Today, Zoe is in college and hopes to study business. She also supports the Network for Teaching Entrepreneurship, an organization that teaches young people in poor communities about business skills like **marketing** and **financing**. She wants to give other kids the same chance she had to start their own businesses.

THREE

Loans

*S*ometimes you just don't have enough money to pay for your business, even if you used all your savings. Luckily, that doesn't mean you have to give up. You have plenty of other options to **fund** your business. One option is to take out a loan.

Loans are borrowed money. They aren't gifts because they have to be paid back to the person you borrowed the money from. Sometimes, your need for money *right now* means you'll have to take out a loan to grow your business.

Signing a contract with the person who loaned you money, even a friend or family member, gives her more confidence that you will pay her back.

Borrowing from Family and Friends

You can choose to take out a loan from people you know personally. Most likely, your family and friends are rooting for your business to succeed. They might be willing to loan you a little money to help you start. Your grandparents, aunts, uncles, cousins, older family friends, or friends your own age are all good places to start. Ask around, but don't be disappointed if people aren't really excited about giving you money. Businesses are risky, and lenders never know for sure if they'll get their money back.

Remember, just because you know the people who loaned you money, doesn't mean you don't need to pay them back. Make it more official by signing a **contract**. Figure out how you're going to make payments. Promise to pay the money back as soon as you start to make a profit, or as soon as you make your first $100. Decide if you're going to pay your lenders back all at once, or if you're going to give them a few dollars at a time until the entire debt is paid off.

You should have a plan for paying your lenders back even if your business doesn't succeed. Businesses are hard to run, and there's always a chance your first business **venture** won't make much money. You'll still need to pay people back. They loaned you money for a short time and expect to get it back.

You can explain the situation to your lenders if your business is struggling to make money. If they're understanding, they might give you more time to pay them back. A good businessperson always pays back debts, though, so don't take more time as a sign you can forget about your debt. Instead, figure out a way to repay.

Applying for a loan requires telling the bank who you are and what you plan on using the loan for. This gives the bank managers the information they need to decide whether they think giving you a loan is a wise investment.

If your parents gave you some money, for example, offer to do more chores around the house to pay back your debt. Or get a part-time job and pay them back a little at a time, a few dollars a week. To pay back friends and other people who loaned you money, you'll probably have to use your personal savings to stay debt-free. Imagine what would happen if you never paid your friend the $30 she loaned you. You would be risking your friendship if you never paid her back!

Taking Out a Bank Loan

Family and friends aren't the only places to get loans. Not everyone you know will happily give you as much money as you need. And if you were starting up a giant, expensive company, your parents probably wouldn't be able to loan you enough.

Banks also offer loans, and they can offer a lot more money than friends and family usually can. Not just anyone can get a bank loan, though. First, and most important for young people, you can't get a loan by yourself if you are under eighteen. You will need a cosigner, someone who is over eighteen and can legally sign a loan contract.

Your cosigner has to be okay taking on the responsibility of the loan. He or she will legally be responsible for paying it back, even if you are the one actually making the money. Your cosigner has to trust you to help pay the loan back. Parents or other older family members are usually the best choice for cosigners.

People who apply for loans at banks also have to have something called good credit. Credit is basically financial trustworthiness. Someone with good credit can be trusted to pay loans back.

Banks do not want to give loans to people who have a history of not paying their loans back. Make sure to pay back the loans you are given in case you ever need to take out a loan in the future.

Someone with bad credit may not be responsible enough to pay back a loan, so the bank will be less likely to give her a loan. People earn credit by paying off credit card bills and by making loan payments on time. You'll want your cosigner to have good credit. Right now, you probably don't have credit if you're under eighteen.

You and your cosigner will have to go to a bank to fill out a loan. Going through the bank where you or your cosigner has a savings or **checking account** is usually a good move.

Loan applications are different depending on the bank you're working with. However, most loan applications will ask you some similar things, like:

- Your reasons for applying for a loan.
- How you will use the loan.
- What you need to buy specifically, and who will you buy it from.
- Whether or not you have other loans and debts, and to whom you owe money.
- Who will be managing the loan.
- Personal information, including addresses, criminal record, and education.

Once you get your loan, you can use the money to start your business. Keep track of how you spend it, and how much you spend.

Eventually you'll have to start paying back your loan. Loans aren't free money! Depending on your loan, you'll have a certain amount of time to pay back your loan, usually one to five years. You'll have to make payments every month. In the end, you'll have to pay back a little more than you borrowed in the first place

Pay back your loan quickly! The longer you wait to pay back a loan, the more you will have to pay the bank in interest.

Business Funding & Finances

because you have to pay interest. The interest is like the price for getting a loan in the first place. You should look for a loan with a low interest rate.

You should also look for loans that let you pay back money faster than the loan period. If your loan is good for two years, but you make so much money that you can pay it back in one, you'll be able to. Then you'll be debt free and won't have to pay any interest during that second year.

SMALL BUSINESS ASSOCIATION LOANS

A part of the government called the Small Business Administration (SBA) helps small businesses throughout the country. The SBA provides information and services for starting and growing small businesses. Part of that is funding small loans for businesses that need them. They are easier to get than some regular bank business loans, and give you a long time to pay them off. Like with other loans, you have to be at least eighteen, or have a cosigner. You'll also still apply for SBA loans through a bank, so ask at your bank if you're interested.

So what does taking out a loan really look like? Well, let's say your graphic design business is doing well. You want to upgrade, though. You're ready for better equipment and better software. The problem is that all that new stuff is really expensive.

At first, you just want to buy a new scanner, which isn't too expensive. You ask your dad for a small loan. He agrees, because he knows you're responsible and can see how hard you've worked at your business. You come up with a plan to pay him back over a few months without any interest.

The new scanner improves your business a little, and you can easily pay your dad back. By now, you can see that you could be doing a lot better work if you had even more new equipment. You really could use some new website design and photo editing software. A high-quality printer and even a new camera would make your business even better. Finally, at the top of your wish list is a new computer that's better suited for graphic design.

You add up how much everything would cost: $5,000! You definitely don't have that much money. You don't think your dad does, either. Should you just give up? Before you decide your business is just too expensive to run, it's time to look into bank loans.

Your dad agrees to be your cosigner, because you were responsible and paid him back when you took out your original loan from him. You go to the bank and talk to an employee who points out a small, $5,000 loan you and your dad can apply for. The bank ends up approving your loan, gives you low interest, and you're all set to go.

You'll need to start paying back the loan over two years, or twenty-four months. Once you buy and start using your new software, computer, and camera, you start charging more for your work. Instead of $50, you charge $75 per job. Your websites look way better than they did before, and you can advertise your higher-quality services. You're making more money than ever, and now you can start paying off your loans right away!

GRANT APPLICATION

Your full name (**exactly as it appears on your Social Security card**)

1. Last name

Your mailing address

4. Number and street (include apt. number)

5. City (and country if not U.S.)

8. Your Social Security Number

FOUR

Grants

Savings and loans are two options you have to finance your business; grants are another. Grants are like gifts of money. Business owners apply for grants, and then receive a check specifically for their business, if they qualify. Unlike loans, you won't need to pay back grants. You are free to use them for your business and then move on.

You can't just use a grant for anything. For example, you can't decide you really want to buy fancy new clothes instead of the new business supplies you won the grant for. You're responsible for using the money for its intended purpose.

Local governments can be a great place to find grant opportunities. Cities and towns want to make sure local businesses succeed, and grants are one way these governemnts help small companies.

Don't get frustrated if you apply for a few grants and don't get them. A lot of people are competing for the same grants, and a lot of people have more experience writing grants than you do. Keep trying! As you get more experience, your grant applications will get better and better. Pretty soon, you'll know exactly how to win a grant, and then you can start using the grant money you win to start or improve your business.

Where to Find Grants

Grants are everywhere if you know where to look. State governments often give out grants to businesses in that state. In general, states want local people to have successful businesses, so they try to help out small business owners with things like loans or grants. Look at the website for your state, and search for grants. You should be able to find quite a few.

City governments also have grants for businesses too. Boston, for example, has a grant program called ReStore Boston, which gives businesses with stores up to $7,000 in grant money to repair and **renovate** storefronts. As you can see, grants can get very specific. Make sure you choose to apply for grants that make sense for your business. You might find grants specifically for advertising graphic design businesses, or grants for starting pet-related businesses. Don't make the mistake of going through a long application process only to find out your business doesn't even qualify for the grant.

The federal government gives out some grants too, but they tend to be for specific businesses. Grants.gov lists all the federal grants you can apply for. State and local governments give out

Grants

No government or organization will grant money to a business it doesn't not think will succeed. Being able to show them an organized and detailed business plan will give others confidence in you and your idea.

Business Funding & Finances

more general grants for starting businesses. **Nonprofits** and even bigger companies also give out grants to small businesses.

You'll even be able to find grants specifically for young people, or for women, or for people of color, or for other groups of people. Organizations who want to support teenage business owners, for example, may offer grants only to teenagers. Another organization might want to encourage Latinos to start businesses, and will grant money to Latino businesspeople. Fewer people will be competing for these more-specific grants, so they're worth checking out.

How to Apply

Because grants are basically free money, lots of people want them! When you apply to get grants, you'll be competing with a lot of other businesspeople who also want the same grant.

You need to stand out on your grant application and do the best job you can. Don't just spend a day on a grant and send in the application at the last second. First, read the application very carefully. You'll need to follow the directions exactly. Ask for help understanding the application if you need it.

You may have to include a business plan in your grant application. Business plans are documents that describe how your business works and what your goals are for your business. A business plan includes the purpose of your business, your marketing plan, estimated profits, and a **cash-flow analysis**. If you don't already have a business plan, you may need to create one to apply for grants.

You'll also need to tell the people giving out the grant why you could use the money. Tell your story! Be specific about what you

Grants 51

will do with the money, and why you are the best business to get the grant.

Think back to the loan you got for your imaginary graphic design business. Instead of that loan you applied for to pay for your new graphic design equipment, you could have chosen to look for grants instead. Back when you decided you needed to buy a new computer, camera, and software, instead you first looked around for small business grants. You spent a long time searching, but eventually you found an arts organization that gives out $5,000 to help people fund creative businesses.

You read over the directions, which look pretty complicated. The deadline for the grant is two months away, so you spend the next two months writing your grant proposal. You create a *résumé*, a business plan, and write out all the details explaining exactly how you will use the grant money. You have lots of people look over your application, and you make a lot of changes to it during those two months. Finally, you're happy with it and send it in.

While you're waiting, you spend time looking for other grants, in case you don't get this one. You end up finding another few grants that give you a similar amount of money. Two are from your state government, and another is from a graphic design company that wants to help other graphic designers start businesses. You apply to all three. This time, applying is a little easier because you know the process. You spend a lot of time on these applications too.

Right after you send in your three applications, you hear back about the first grant you applied for—you didn't get it. You're a little sad, but you realize it was your first time applying for a grant and you might not have really gotten the hang of it yet. After a few more weeks, you hear back from the other grants you applied to. You got one of the government grants! Your hard work paid off, and you've become a successful grant writer. Now you can pay for your new equipment, and you don't even have to worry about paying back a loan. All that hard work applying to grants was worth the effort.

Grants in Real Life

Young people can take advantage of grants. Just ask Anshul Samar, the inventor of a chemistry board game called Elementeo. As a young teen, Anshul spent a few years creating and developing his board game, which first started selling in 2008.

Anshul wanted his board game to be a big deal. He didn't want just a few people playing it—he wanted the whole country playing it! He needed the money to match his goal.

"When I was in sixth grade, I applied for a grant," Anshul explains. "I didn't even ask my dad for anything. The California Association for the Gifted gave me $500. It was like my pre-pre-*seed funding*. That $500 is what got me going for the next two years. It would have been very hard to start this without someone trusting me, a thirteen-year-old, with $500."

The $500 grant got Anshul started, and even kept him going for two years! After that, he realized he needed some more money to truly make his game great. He borrowed some from his dad, who is also an *entrepreneur* like Anshul. He understood how important money is to start businesses, so he loaned his son some.

Anshul Samar started his business with only a $500 grant. In 2009 he was awarded $25,000 by the Davidson Institute for Elementeo, money that is helping his business grow even larger.

Business Funding & Finances

CROWDFUNDING

The Internet has opened up lots of possibilities for funding businesses. One way you can raise money to start or grow your business is through crowdfunding websites. The idea behind crowdfunding sites is to get a little bit of money from a lot of people. Asking hundreds or even thousands of people to help you start a business isn't so hard on the Internet. Websites like Kickstarter or Indiegogo make it easy. Just sign up for an account on a crowdfunding website. You'll need to set up a page for your business, where you explain why you're asking for money, and what your financial goals are. The more convincing you are, the more money you'll get. Once you start up your page, you can send e-mails to people you know, who can then tell other people they know, and so on. You'll probably get people you've never even met giving you money!

Anshul learned the value of small grants to start businesses. He says, "It's true that if you don't have money, it's hard to do anything." He goes on to describe his plan to set up his own grant-giving organization. "That's actually one of my personal goals, as an entrepreneur. There are a lot of youth in the world with an idea. They don't have someone to believe in them, and they don't have the money to do it. A lot of people out there don't have encouragement. I want to give $500, $1,000, $2,000 grants to youth around the world . . . $500 can take you a lot of places. You just need that *catalyst* to get you started."

Young people like Anshul Samar and Zoe Damacela have learned how important money is for starting a business. Instead

VENTURE CAPITAL

Yet another way to fund your business is with something called venture capital. Venture capital is money given by people who are willing to fund your business in return for sharing in the profits when the business becomes successful. If you receive venture capital, that means the people who gave you money really think your business could make a lot of money and reach a lot of people. Accepting venture capital means you'll get a lot of money and can really focus on making your business a success. Accepting venture capital also means letting someone else have partial control of your business. You might not even make any money until the people who gave you venture capital have profited from your business.

Anshul Samar explored getting venture capital. "VCs [venture capitalists] did contact us, and we must have had a half-dozen meetings," Anshul said. The VCs had different ideas about the business in the end, and Anshul decided not to work with them. "We wanted to go at our own pace. We knew, if you take VC, you're working sixty hours a week and going at a very fast pace. At that time, with school, we wanted to go slow." Doing well in school is important to Anshul, and he didn't want to sacrifice his grades and learning for his business.

Business Funding & Finances

of giving up and letting go of their business dreams, they worked hard to get the money they needed.

Whether you use personal savings, ask your family for money, get a bank loan, or apply for a grant, you have so many choices for starting up your own business and helping it grow. And with some good business decisions, you'll soon be making the money you spent transform into money you're making!

Find Out More

ONLINE

7 Small Business Ideas for Teenagers & Kids
www.moneycrashers.com/business-ideas-teenagers-kids

Investopedia
www.investopedia.com/university/small-business/financing-your-
business.asp

SBA.gov: Find Loans, Grants, & Other Assistance
www.sba.gov/content/find-business-loans-grants-other-financial-
assistance

TeachingKidsBusiness.com: Finance
www.teachingkidsbusiness.com/business-basics-finance.htm

In Books

Bateman, Katherine R. *The Young Investor: Projects and Activities for Making Your Money Grow*. Chicago, Ill.: Chicago Review Press, 2010.

Bernstein, Daryl. *Better Than a Lemonade Stand! Small Business Ideas for Kids*. New York: Aladdin, 2012.

Chatzky, Jean. *Not Your Parents' Money Book: Making, Saving, and Spending Your Own Money*. New York: Simon and Schuster, 2010.

Vocabulary

Adamant: refusing to change one's mind.

Cash-flow analysis: a comparison of how much money you are spending and when, with how much money you are making and when you will be making it.

Catalyst: a person or thing that causes something to happen.

Checking account: money kept in a bank that can be easily used to pay for things; money that can be taken from the bank using an ATM, check, or debit card.

Contract: a written agreement that is enforceable by law.

Debts: money owed to another person or to a bank or company.

Effectively: capable of producing a result quickly.

Entrepreneur: a person who takes risks to set up a business.

Estimate: a guess.

Financing: managing money.

Fund: to pay for.

Income: money received on a regular basis for work.

Interest: money paid regularly in return for the use of that money, or for delaying the payment of a debt.

Investment: the act of giving money, time, or energy to a particular project, in return for a benefit.

Marketing: the way a business sells a product by telling people about it.

Nonprofits: organizations whose goal is to make money for a stated purpose, often to help people or to achieve some good cause, rather than to earn money for the owners.

Passionate: having strong feelings about something.

Professional: businesslike and appropriate.

Seed Funding: money used to start a new company.

Self-Employed: working for yourself.

Service: a task one group or person performs to help another group or person, often for money.

Taxes: money paid to the government for the services they provide the people of the country or state.

Renovate: to change or remake for the better.

Résumé: a document that explains why you are the best fit for a new job as well as your past work experience.

Venture: something you attempt with out knowing the outcome.

Wages: money paid for time worked.

Index

advertising 18, 21, 49
applications 13, 41, 49, 52

bank 7–8, 25, 27, 38–39, 41–44, 57
budget 20–22
business plan 7, 26, 50–52

checking account 41
classes 14
corporation 14
cosigner 39, 41, 43–44
crowdfunding 55
customers 7–9, 17–21, 23, 26

Damacela, Zoe 30–31, 55
domain name 13, 15, 17–18

employees 8, 26

family 36–37, 39, 57

government 13, 18–19, 43, 49–50, 52–53
grants 5, 47–49, 51–53, 55
graphic design 15, 18–19, 21, 44, 49, 52

income 18
interest 29, 42–44

licenses 13–14
loans 35, 39–41, 43–45, 47, 49

marketing 33, 51
materials 13, 17, 26

nonprofits 51

on-going costs 17, 21

Samar, Anshul 53–56
savings 5, 29, 35, 39, 41, 47, 57
startup costs 13, 15, 17, 21, 27–29, 33
stores 49

taxes 8, 14, 18–19, 21, 27

venture capital 56

website 13, 15–16, 18, 21, 23, 44, 49, 55

About the Author and Consultant

C.F. Earl is a writer living and working in Binghamton, New York. Earl writes mostly on social and historical topics, including health, the military, and finances.

Brigitte Madrian is the Aetna Professor of Public Policy and Corporate Management at the Harvard Kennedy School. Before coming to Harvard in 2006, she was on the faculty at the University of Pennsylvania Wharton School (2003–2006), the University of Chicago Graduate School of Business (1995–2003) and the Harvard University Economics Department (1993–1995). She is also a research associate and co-director of the Household Finance working group at the National Bureau of Economic Research. Dr. Madrian received her PhD in economics from the Massachusetts Institute of Technology and studied economics as an undergraduate at Brigham Young University. She is the recipient of the National Academy of Social Insurance Dissertation Prize (first place, 1994) and a two-time recipient of the TIAA-CREF Paul A. Samuelson Award for Scholarly Research on Lifelong Financial Security (2002 and 2011).

Picture Credits